Mood Stabilizer

Jolynn Wlasiuk

Presentation by *BookLeaf Publishing*

Web: www.bookleafpub.com

E-mail: info@bookleafpub.com

ISBN: 9789358367232

First edition 2023

A life worth living...

Memory Lane

I seldom take that turn down memory lane
There's no stopping them once they start.
The memories come flooding in like a dam
released for summer-
Like the dam near where we buried my mother.
And I think that proves my point.

Darkness

I remember feeling cold,
I remember the tightness in my chest.
The dark had come before,
Just never quite like this.
I tried to sleep it off,
My mind just wouldn't rest.
Not used to feeling everything
Then nothing all at once.

Just a Girl

Just a girl, born in the heat of summer
Just a girl, one night would change her future
Just a girl, mind full of what if's and wonders
Just a girl, an entire world to discover
Just a girl, who finally found her other
Just a bride, a bride without her mother

Dreams

I dreamed of you beside me
We sat down on the dock.
A warm breeze embraced us,
Not worried about a clock.
The waves crashed against our feet,
As you sat there beside me.
We said the things we never said,
And then we fell in love again.

A Life to Live

My depression was never one for seclusion.
It was an adrenaline-seeking, weed-smoking,
busy-living delusion.
It even made its way to work each day.
You see, depression isn't always dark rooms and
bouts of isolation.
It has a life to live too.

Nobody's Child

I have always seen myself as "Nobody's Child."
Surrounded by pitied faces
With no expectations that I'd even go places.
The world just let me wander
No one to make proud
I made my own path, got lost, but never found.
An invisible being, alone in the wild,
And forever,
Nobody's child.

All the Things You'd Say

I don't write of you much. Somedays I know I
should.
Like when you visit me in my dreams at night, I
really wish I would.
I think of you while driving, of all the things
you'd say.
Unconditional love that screams you're proud of
me.

Never Been Home

They say, these small towns are the places to be
But you know why I don't believe it?

Through all of the good memories and all of the
bad,
This place has never seemed like home to me.
It's dragging me down and holding me back.
Constant reminders of everything I lack:
Happiness, family, a reason to live, or a reason
to leave.
So maybe it's time for a change.
Somewhere the night fading into day won't feel
so strange.
Someplace my mind won't feel so heavy
Won't make me feel this alone

Damn, this place has never been home.

His Perspective

Her eyes held the universe
Her voice to me was gold
I never knew the pain she'd seen
Her weakness never showed
Now I've met her darkness
It stopped by and settled in
The two of us
We're stuck in time
Until she loves herself again

MDD & PTSD

MDD, BPD, ADHD, PTSD
Too many lives depending on the ABCs
To end their struggles
Doctors use codes and puzzles
To tell us which pills to take
Hell, it's only our lives at stake

Fatal Difference

Perhaps that was our fatal difference
I believe in second chances
And you're afraid of risks

Internal Struggle

Self-sabotage became part of my being
A subconscious storm that's always been
brewing
All too often I blur the lines
Between dancing beneath the stars
And ruining the evening completely

Adrenaline Seeker

Nothing scared her more than the dark
But nothing intrigued her more than death
She'd be on the verge of a breakdown
And go skydiving instead

Unraveled

His lies began unraveling,
Until the truth tangled about my feet.
My vision started to blur,
And I could no longer speak.

Anomaly

I could tell you stories
Of tragically broken things
But when it comes to you and me
You're an anomaly.
Someone who wants to stay
And never lets me doubt.
You're everything I can't seem to write about.

It's Over

You won't find closure, no matter where you
look.
Not within a song, or at the end of a book.
You won't find it at the bottom of the bottle,
Or even after the last line you took.

Broken Pieces

I know you see chaos, when you look into my
eyes.
I hope you don't notice, but it's not something I
hide.
The world has left me damaged, I've tried to fix
what broke.
I don't need you to save me, just a little hope.

What Is

Maybe we aren't meant to understand
The things that are no longer meant for us.
Even if they vanish,
With no sound or no trace.
I think we're meant to accept what was,
In place of what could be or
could've been.

Shipwrecked

This pain is anchored to my soul
And I'm shipwrecked-
On an island of misery.
I rebuilt this heart from
Stick and stone
But damn, your words still hurt me.

One Day More

There are days I find hope within my reach
Stretching far, an endless beach.
I move forward quietly, a humble gift
I promise myself one day more, I'll persist.
I tell myself the way is clear
And for today I have no fear.

Eyes Wide Open

It was an ordinary day for me, I think. Actually,
no.
I felt the fog rolling in for months.
I thought I had a grip this time but suddenly it
slipped.
It stripped me of my worth this time, my
confidence, and belonging.
It never let me sleep, left with intrusive thoughts
that haunted me till morning.
Even on those tolling nights, I held on tight and
hoped that dawn was coming.
I'd say I hit rock bottom, but I woke up and saw
the ground approaching.